Social Media for

Teachers and Healers

The Essential Guide to
Growing Your Network
without Losing Your Zen

By Darren Main

Dedicated to Jesse Dornan

Although your time on this earth was far too short, I will be forever grateful that I had the chance to work with you and that your voice will live on in many of my audiobooks.

Table of Contents

Introduction

On a cold rainy night in the winter of 2005, a young man approached me after yoga class. He had been taking my class for a while and was always very friendly. Up until that conversation, however, I had never chatted with him at length, but he had a welcoming smile and a warm personality.

Normally, when people approach me after class, it is to ask me about an injury or to tell me about an experience they had while practicing. But I was so taken aback by the unexpected nature of this conversation. He explained that he was part of a small startup company that was ready to launch and suggested I get on the bandwagon. His company was called Twitter.

"Silly name for a company," I thought.

He explained that microblogging would be the wave of the future and that it was a perfect opportunity for a yoga teacher to communicate with existing students and potential students who had not yet tried my class.

"Microblogging will never catch on," I mused, while smiling politely.

I would like to tell you that I went home, reflected on the conversation, and saw the future in a mystical vision gained from my yoga and meditation practice. I would like to tell you that I jumped on the opportunity to start tweeting before anyone knew what Twitter was. Unfortunately, I didn't give Twitter another thought for several more years.

Honestly, I became a yoga teacher and a massage therapist so that I could avoid sitting in front of a computer all day. In time, however, I decided to give social networking a try. I started with a Facebook account and then added in Twitter. I've used other social media platforms as well. Shockingly, I have found a genuine appreciation for social media. In an unexpected way, I have found that social media can be an amazing extension of my work as a modern teacher.

Whether you are a yoga teacher, massage therapist, chiropractor, or psychotherapist, the essence of what you do is rooted in healing, and all healing is about relationships. The modalities may change, but the essence of what we do is form relationships with those we serve. It is in these relationships that true and lasting healing occurs. Our ability to connect with and deepen relationships with existing and potential students and clients makes social networking a natural fit. It can become an extension of what we already do if pursued mindfully and ethically.

In 2009, I published the first edition of *The Yogi Entrepreneur: A Guide to Earning a Mindful Living Through Yoga.* In that book, I mentioned social media such as Facebook and Twitter as helpful marketing tools. By the time the second edition of the book came out, social networking had become essential and received a lot more attention when I revised the book.

In 2017, I released the third edition of that same book. Again, many updates were made, and I considered having an entire chapter devoted to social media. As I sat to write that new chapter, I quickly realized that the content of that chapter was much more extensive than a few short pages could accommodate. Rather than attempting to cram lots of information into one chapter within a larger book, I decided to write the book you are reading right now.

About This Book

The first few chapters of this book will focus on social media platforms in a very general way. While every platform is different, they all have fundamental things in common. Of course, some will lend themselves to your personality and your work more than others, so rather than trying to have a presence on every social network, I recommend you choose the ones that speak to your needs and interests. Learning the fundamentals will give you the ability to pick and choose in an informed way.

The last three chapters of this book will focus specifically on Facebook, Twitter and Instagram. These networks are by far the biggest and perhaps the most important. Because of their prominence, I felt it was important to do a deeper dive into the services they offer and how to navigate the richness of each platform.

In addition to this book, I host a popular Facebook group called the Yogi Entrepreneur. Although it began as a place for yoga teachers to network, we welcome healers of every discipline. It is a wonderful place to network with other healing professionals and get marketing advice and support from other teachers and healers. You can find this Facebook group at
www.facebook.com/groups/YogiEntrepreneur

So take a deep breath, do your best to let go of preconceptions and fears about social media, and let's get started.

Darren Main
www.darrenmain.com

Chapter One:

The Resistance Movement

Chances are you're reading this book begrudgingly. You've known for years that you need to up your social media game, but if you're like most teachers and healers, you have resisted. Perhaps you don't even have a Facebook page or a Twitter feed. Or maybe you have these things but rarely, if ever, post updates.

Perhaps you resist social media with every fiber in your being. Perhaps you don't see the point, or maybe you don't think you have the time to invest in it. Maybe you enjoy social media on a personal level, but you don't want it to bleed into your work life. Or maybe you're concerned about privacy.

Whatever your reasons, you are not alone in being a part of what I call the Resistance Movement. I know a lot about this because I was a card-carrying member of the Resistance Movement for a very long time. But once I learned how to manage social media in a way that was fun, effective, and—most of all— took very little of my time, I actually started to change my point of view. In fact, I've come to the point where social media is almost as satisfying as teaching a yoga class because I now see it as an extension of my teaching.

To get you to this point, I have a favor to ask and a promise to make. First, the favor. I want you to trust me at least until you try a few of the techniques in this book. I don't believe blind faith is a healthy thing, but I also don't believe a closed mind is fertile ground for growth. If you are not ready to leave the Resistance Movement after reading this book and trying some of the techniques within these pages, I will be very surprised.

What I'm asking of you is that you trust me for one month. Simply try the techniques in this book for one month and then evaluate the results. If you are not happy with the results, you never have to post anything to social media again. If you are satisfied with the results, however, you may have found something truly amazing to augment the work and marketing efforts you are already doing.

My promise to you is that I will provide you with the tools you need to have a social media presence that is rewarding and dramatically helps your marketing and branding efforts. I promise that you will not need to devote more than one hour per week and that you are guaranteed to see results, including a growing client base, more consistency from existing clients, and an improved ability to educate and inspire the people you serve.

I'm going to be honest with you. Numbers and statistics make me go cross eyed. I'm just not a numbers guy. And yet the statistics on social media make my eyes pop. I'll keep the statistics to a minimum, but it is important to realize the significance and potential of these platforms.

Consider Facebook for a moment. In 2018, it was estimated that nearly two billion people engaged with Facebook in some way every single day. They may check messages on their phone, they may like a post, or they may post pictures of their family. They may share news or learn about a product or event. That is a truly staggering number.

Twitter has over 330 million active users every single month. It has become a major source of news and information for a huge percentage of the population in developed countries and even some countries that are still developing.

And of course, there are other channels as well. In fact, it's estimated that over 80% of Americans have at least one social media account.

The reason I'm giving you all these numbers is to underscore just what an opportunity social media is.

Take a moment and consider the teachers and healers you have worked with over the years—all the yoga teachers, meditation teachers, clergy members, massage therapists, chiropractors, and other healers. How did you find them? What convinced you to trust them in the first place? Some of them you may have found by accident. Perhaps their yoga class fit your schedule, or maybe the massage therapist was running a promotion. But I would be willing to bet a large percentage of the people you work with were introduced to you by your circle of friends.

Social influence is nothing new. People have been connecting friends and family with the services and products since the dawn of time. More often than not, the glossy magazine or flashy car commercial, while influential in your decision-making, is not the deciding factor. More likely, seeing and hearing about products and services from those in your social circles will influence your decisions more.

What social media networks do is harness this simple principle. By connecting people based on relationships, interests, organizations (like schools and workplaces), and other data points, like-minded people can connect and share information. Sometimes the information is relatively useless in the broader scheme of things, but often times it can influence the decisions people make about which yoga class to take or which chiropractor can help with an injured back.

As a teacher or healer, if you are not taking advantage of this powerful tool for branding and marketing, you are at a decided disadvantage. All of the skill and knowledge in the world is only as good as the people you can reach. The primary way we reach people in today's marketplace is through social media.

The nice thing about social media, especially when compared to more traditional forms of marketing, is it is mostly organic. Social media marketing is an extension of a natural conversation that occurs on each platform. The difference between Twitter, Facebook, Instagram, and other platforms is largely cosmetic. The underlying principles are largely the same. People want to share and various social networks facilitate that sharing.

Why Resist?

When I'm coaching yoga teachers, I often ask why they don't have a Facebook page or a Twitter feed. The answers are often predictable. Some bemoan the lack of human contact that occurs when people spend too much time on social media. Others have a fear of technology or simply feel overwhelmed at the prospect of building a following. Still, others enjoy teaching yoga so much that they simply don't want to waste time in front of a computer screen.

The truth is these are reasonable positions and concerns. In fact, I can relate to them entirely. But what I have come to learn is that it's not an either/or proposition. The human contact that people experience in one of my yoga classes can only happen if people know the class exists. Through social media, I can educate people about the power of yoga to transform their health, state of mind, and their ability to connect with others in a more compassionate way.

Mother Teresa was once asked why she chose Calcutta. Her answer was simple: "That is where the poorest of the poor live." Mother Teresa may have been called to live and work in Calcutta, but chances are you are called to live in your local community. But Mother Teresa's simple wisdom extends to teachers and healers everywhere. It is not enough to print some business cards and call yourself a healer or roll out a yoga mat and call yourself a teacher. We need to go to where the people are. And if the statistics above are any indication, social media platforms like Facebook and Twitter are the new centers of social influence.

Another thing to consider is that technology, while potentially harmful, can also be healing. It can bring ideas and people together in ways never imagined even 20 years ago. It can also make this process easier and less time-consuming.

Once you learn the techniques in this book, you'll realize that it takes surprisingly little time to engage with your audience and build a following on whatever networks you choose. In fact, I predict you will be spending less than one hour per week on your social media efforts once you are up and running. Best of all, it requires almost no technical expertise whatsoever. You simply need to commit a little bit of time and a little bit of effort.

Chapter Two:

Social Media Branding

For years, I was afraid of branding. It struck me as the type of thing capitalists did in boardrooms to get people to buy sugary soft drinks, makeup, and widgets they did not need. To a certain extent that is true. But branding is really much bigger than all of that, and whether or not you know it, you already have a brand.

Many people falsely believe that a brand is your logo and the colors and fonts you use on your website and in print. But branding is so much more. A brand is what people think and feel about you and your work. It is what people say about you when you're not in the room. You have a personal brand with your friends and family, and you also have a brand associated with your professional persona as a healer or teacher.

Some parts of your brand are obvious. For example, I'm a yoga teacher, and I focus on making the philosophical aspects of yoga more user-friendly and understandable to the average yoga practitioner. I'm also known for my work in the HIV community and with cancer patients and those diagnosed with autoimmune diseases. But my brand also encompasses things like my sense of humor, the space I hold for people when they take my class, and how people feel when they leave my class versus how they felt when they first walked in. My brand is defined by the way I present myself to the world, and increasingly it is defined by the things I post on social media too.

As I noted, everyone has a brand. It's as if the universe gave each of us a plot of land. On that plot of land, you can plant pumpkins, carrots, apple trees, a variety of fruits and vegetables, or anything you want. You can also neglect the plot of land and allow weeds to take over. The choice is yours. What grows on that plot of land is akin to your personal and professional brands. The question then becomes:do you want to cultivate your brand, or do you want to let your brand just sort of happen?" Or, to ask it another way, do you want your brand to be a productive and well-maintained garden or a patch of weeds?

In this chapter, I would like to explore your social media branding. This will be done in two separate but related ways. The first will focus on the obvious branding we do by choosing graphics, photos, and other assets associated with each social media platform. Then we will turn our attention to other types of branding. Everything you post on Twitter, Facebook, Instagram, etc. will help to define your brand as a teacher or healer, for better or worse. I'm hoping this chapter will help you to think carefully about the things you post so that you can cultivate a brand worthy of the healing work you do.

The All-Important Profile

There are some very basic things you can do to establish a brand right out of the gate. In every social media network, you will have the opportunity to post basic information about who you are, how people can learn more about your work, where your business is located, and other basic details.

A surprising number of people don't take the time to fill out the profile on their social media accounts. To be clear, each social media account will be a little bit different—some will have more options than others, and some will have options tailored to the specific platform—but filling out as much of each profile as possible will help the right people find you and learn more about the healing work you offer. To skip this most basic step is to cut yourself off at the knees. In the next chapter, we will talk about various social networks and how they use complex algorithms to match like-minded people with friends and businesses to whom they will likely relate well. Your profile goes a long way in refining the accuracy of those algorithms.

Let's look at a simple example. Suppose Jennifer has just graduated from massage school. She is excited to get started seeing new clients and is spreading the word about the healing work she is offering. She has launched a website, chosen several social networks on which she will promote herself, and opened a small massage office in Cambridge, Massachusetts.

No matter how good Jennifer is at massage therapy or how healing her hands may be, it is unlikely that someone from Los Angeles is going to seek her out unless they happen to be visiting Cambridge on a business trip or vacation. Even more, potential customers may not know what sets Jennifer apart from other massage therapists. Not every massage therapist is the same. Some do Shiatsu while others offer Swedish massage. Some will do deep pressure massage and others will do energy work.

If somebody is interested in Jennifer's work after seeing her Facebook post, they will likely want to know where her office is and what type of work she offers. Getting this information will be needlessly difficult if she has not filled out her profile completely. In addition, when people search for a specific service—especially one that is location dependent, like massage therapy, her profile would not likely appear in searches if she did not include the address of her studio.

Let's take a moment and look at some of the key data points that should be included in any profile. This will help potential students and clients locate you and hopefully find their way to your class or office.

Name

The most obvious data point is your name. As a healer or a teacher, your name is intimately associated with your brand. Many teachers and healers attempt to get cute with this. While it is fine to have a brand name for your business, not putting your first and last name on your profile or fan page is a good way to be overlooked entirely.

It is also worth considering what name you will use. For example, a doctor might want to use a full name complete with initials documenting their studies. A yoga teacher, on the other hand, may want to use a shortened name or Sanskrit name, as yoga tends to be more casual.

Location

Entering location information into your profile is essential if you are a location-based healer or teacher. For almost everyone reading this book, you will be associated with the town or city in which you work. There are some exceptions to this rule. For example, I write books and offer trainings all over the world. Therefore, my brand is not exclusively a San Francisco brand but rather an international brand. My goal is to reach out to people in a very wide geographical circle.

But like most people, you probably offer massage, chiropractic, and yoga classes and other forms of teaching and healing in your local neighborhood. If you live in a larger city, that may be a neighborhood within the city. If you live in a smaller town, you probably practice in the city or town where you live.

Consider this. Someone is on Twitter looking for a chiropractor in Washington, DC. If you have filled out your profile completely with your postal code or the name of your city and state, there is a good chance your Twitter feed will pop up in a search of chiropractors in Washington, DC. If, however, you leave this field blank, there will be no way for people to find you.

Website

Many teachers and healers use a social media network or a collection of networks as replacement for a traditional website. In my opinion, this is a mistake. Your website offers the opportunity to really introduce yourself and your work to people in a much more detailed way. People can really get a feel for who you are and what you do. They can see testimonials from students and clients who have benefited from your work, and they can find your schedule of events, classes, and appointment availability.

If you have a website, and I strongly suggest that you do, be sure to post it in the profile section of all your social media networks. This will allow people to quickly learn more about you, if they're intrigued or interested, after reading something you posted. If people can't easily get more information, they will likely be onto the next thing that catches their eye, and your efforts will be greatly diminished.

Workplace

Most social media platforms allow you to list the places you work. This is really important if you offer your healing work or classes at a spa, gym, or studio. If, for example, a person works at the YMCA, and they list that on their profile, anyone searching for yoga teachers at the local YMCA will find your profile. This can help you promote your class at the YMCA, but it also helps you to build your mailing list, invite people to take classes you offer in other venues, and to connect with them outside of the yoga studio or gym.

The Call to Action (CTA)

Perhaps the most important feature that all social media platforms offer, though in admittedly different ways, is the call to action, or CTA. Ultimately, we want the people who visit our profile to do something. We want them to book a massage or chiropractic session, come in for counseling, or join us on a yoga retreat. A call to action is the mechanism by which they take that step.

Not everyone is going to take a class or book a session with you after visiting your Facebook page just once. But if articles and inspirational posts on your fan page have piqued their interest several times, they may be ready to take the next step—booking a session or taking a class.

As you fill in your profile, you should be clear about what your CTA is going to be. Ideally, it's what you want visitors or followers to do. In my case, my hope is that they will eventually take a class with me, attend a workshop or retreat, or buy one of my books. After all, that's how I put food on the table.

Deciding on your CTA and then embedding that message into your profile will smooth the transition to make an interested follower on social media into a paying customer. Some networks allow you to use buttons to join a mailing list, purchase products, visit a website, or even register for an event. Some will even allow you to book appointments right through the platform itself. While each platform is a bit different, finding out what the CTA options are and then choosing something that is best suited for you and your business is an important tool when converting followers into paying customers. In today's fast-paced world, anything more than the click of a button is likely going to fail. You need to make it easy for customers to make the leap from following to acting.

Graphics and Photos

Most social media platforms will enable you to have a few standard photos or graphics that brand your page. Most will include a headshot or logo as well as a cover photo. For almost all teachers and healers, you're better off using a headshot so that people can feel familiar with you as a person, though some people may put their logo in this space.

Cover photos can be a bit more tricky. Each platform requires different dimensions. But the cover photo is very important. It sets the tone for the user experience as they spend time on your page or review your posts. You may choose something more neutral like a nature scene that evokes a sense of calm. Other people may put a picture of their yoga class or their massage room as a cover photo. This helps potential students and clients envision themselves experiencing your work. Still, others put a picture of themselves in action—maybe assisting a student, demonstrating a pose, or putting their hands on somebody's back while on a massage table.

Think carefully about the photos you choose to post. What you post will dramatically affect your brand. Branding is, in large part, emotional. Ask yourself, "How does this photo make me feel?" By understanding how a photo or graphic makes you feel, you will understand the effect it will likely have on the people that visit your social media page.

TIP

Having a tasteful cover photo created is very affordable on services like Fiverr.com. You can even request the cover image size for the various networks on which you are posting. Having a cover photo professionally designed will add credibility to your brand and save hours of time.

The Click-Bait Dilemma

It's not hard to get something to go viral on the internet. If you want a lot of people to click on something, simply post something shocking, funny, or offensive. But not all click bait is good. The fact that you got an offensive statement to go viral will not necessarily increase the number of people who come to you for a treatment or participate in your class.

One of the key mistakes people make is believing that all attention is good attention. Nothing could be further from the truth. Having a post go viral is wonderful. Nothing spreads the word about your powerful healing work like a well-crafted post that many people share and like. But such posts need to further your narrative and reinforce your brand rather than distracting from that goal.

Luckily, we will be discussing how to make posts more likely to be shared, liked, and commented on in the next chapter. You don't have to sink to the bottom of the barrel to get people to engage with the content you post.

You simply have to know how to post wisely so that people are more interested in engaging with your content.

Questions for Contemplation

The following questions should be carefully considered and reflected upon. The more you reflect on the questions listed below, the better you will be at crafting your narrative and sharing your story on social media. One of the fatal mistakes most teachers and healers make is not carefully considering what their narrative is going to be. This leads to a bunch of social media posts that can either distract from or contradict the narrative you hope to present to the world.

Of course, the answers to these questions may change over time. As you grow in your teaching or healing practice, you may find new aspects to the work you offer. Your focus may change, or you may discover something about yourself that is worth noting that you hadn't considered previously. Even if your answers to the following questions are incomplete today, you need to start somewhere. Take some time right now to consider each of these questions. Perhaps write out the answers. A small amount of time invested in this simple practice now will yield incredible results for you later on.

- What is your current brand? What do people say about your work when you are not around?
- What would you like your brand to be? What would you like people to say about you when you are not around?
- What elements of your personal story would create a compelling narrative?
- What types of posts, images, videos will reinforce your brand and narrative?

- What types of posts, images, videos will distract from or damage your brand and narrative?

Ten Hacks for Developing Your Brand

Become an Expert

One of the best ways you can brand yourself is to become an expert. Become the person people look to for advice when they have a specific need. Perhaps you're a massage therapist that works with pregnant women. Or maybe you are a qigong teacher that helps hyperactive children learn to self-regulate. Maybe your yoga practice helped you to recover from your addiction. Or perhaps you have a passion for helping the Jewish community integrate meditation into their existing belief system.

We all have something we are passionate and knowledgeable about, and that makes us stand out. Find out what your expertise is, and then brand yourself accordingly. Thankfully, social media makes this process very easy.

Through social media you can share articles, videos, inspiring tips and hints, and other content that will encourage your students and clients to see you as an expert. Ideally, some of the content you share will be produced by you. Perhaps you'll write an article for your blog or produce a video on YouTube. But much of the content you can share can be curated from other sources. I will provide more information on how to curate quality content in another chapter.

Know Your Audience

It may seem like a no-brainer, but knowing your audience is essential. Imagine if a college professor skilled in teaching graduate students used the same voice, tone, and techniques with grade school students. The content you share and the way you communicate with the members of your social networks should be governed in large part by your intended audience.

It would not make much sense for a prenatal yoga teacher to post articles about prostate cancer. But if you teach meditation in grade schools, it probably makes sense to post articles that would appeal to teachers and parents rather than Buddhist monks. If your target audience for massage is senior citizens, posting videos with young athletes getting bodywork is not going to catch their eye. Before you post anything to one of your networks, ask yourself whether the post will speak to and be heard by your target audience.

Define Your Narrative

Above we discussed the profile and other obvious branding tools at your disposal on various social media platforms. These are essential and important things to consider. But what is even more important is the narrative that you create about your work.

Everyone has a story. The facets in your personal story are diverse and varied. Perhaps you're married and have children, or perhaps you're single and carefree. Maybe you grew up wealthy, or maybe you come from extreme poverty. Perhaps you've had a sickness or an injury that challenged you but ultimately made you stronger. Or maybe you have a religious, ethnic, or racial background that helps define who you are as a teacher or healer.

Each and every one of us has more qualities than we could possibly count. We have good days and bad days. We have strengths and weaknesses. We have qualities for which we are proud and those for which we are ashamed. It would be impossible to share every quality with the world, and even if we could, it would not be advisable. Your narrative is the story you tell. It is the picking and choosing of various qualities to create a compelling story.

It is not enough to simply tell a story. You need to recognize that everything you post contributes to your narrative. This is either to your benefit or to your detriment. Deciding what your narrative will be and then posting things that bolster that narrative is essential. It is also essential that you avoid posting things that distract from that narrative.

For example, you may have strong political opinions, but will it serve your narrative to post them publicly? If your narrative is to be an even-tempered, open-hearted person that welcomes everyone, is posting about what a jerk the president is going to further your goals? It may be true that you feel that way, and it may feel good to post it, but does it further your goal of weaving a narrative about creating a safe, stress-free environment for healing and personal growth?

It is essential to have this conversation with yourself before you start posting everything that crosses your mind. This is not to say that you cannot have strong opinions or a multifaceted life. But the fastest way to turn people off is to overshare in a way that distracts from your narrative. You don't need to be strategic or manipulative and plan out the things you want to share. But if you simply take a moment before you hit the post button to ask, "Will this post complement or distract from my narrative?" you will have much greater success in engaging your audience and helping them to feel like they know you on a much deeper level.

Your narrative should always be true, but that doesn't mean it can't be also be cultivated. One way to understand narratives is to look at various US presidents.

Bill Clinton was born in Hope, Arkansas. His early life was difficult, and he did not have much in the way of material advantages. Over and over again, he would talk about being the boy from Hope. The narrative—even someone coming from a small town with limited resources could do great things in the United States.

George W. Bush had a very different narrative. He branded himself as a compassionate conservative informed by his Christian beliefs, which he portrayed as being someone who espoused traditional conservative values while lifting up the marginalized. Throughout his campaigning and presidency, he would tell stories and answer questions in interviews that reaffirmed his narrative of being a compassionate conservative.

When Barack Obama was running for president and all through his eight years as president, he would frequently start speaking by saying, "Only in America is a story like mine possible. . . " His narrative of hope and faith in the American Dream was even compelling and uplifting to many who didn't vote for him. He used details from his personal life to make himself more relatable to the average American. If you want to succeed as a teacher or healer, you need to do the same thing.

All three presidents were very different. Some you may have voted for and others perhaps not. The point is they had a story to tell, and they would hammer that story home at every opportunity. Eventually the details of their biographies became part of their brand. It's not that they were lying or saying something that was not true. They were simply redirecting you, the potential voter, to specific aspects of their lives so that you would feel more comfortable voting for them.

When you post to social media, you are contributing to or distracting from your narrative. You are either muddying the waters or you're underlining and highlighting the narrative you want people to recognize. This point cannot be overstated. For better or worse, what you post to social media will always add to or distract from the brand and narrative you are trying to create and cultivate.

For example, imagine a qigong teacher named Edward wants to brand his classes as a space where people can find refuge from the storms of the world. He posts inspiring articles, beautiful images of people practicing qigong, inspirational videos, and the occasional announcement about workshops and classes he is offering.

Like most people, Edward is interested in making the world a better place and uses politics as a vehicle to do that. But he has strong political views and is not shy about expressing those views with his friends and family. There's nothing wrong with this, of course, but when he starts posting his political opinions to his professional social media pages, his brand quickly becomes tainted.

Politics can be toxic in any conversation. Some people who read Edward's posts will agree with him, but feel the agitation that comes with thinking about the evening news. Other people will disagree with his political point of view and may not come to his class. In either case, he is distracting from his brand. Rather than thinking of his class as a refuge, people may feel subtle or perhaps not-so-subtle levels of anxiety—the exact opposite of the brand he had hoped to cultivate.

To be clear, there's nothing wrong with posting something about a political cause for which you are passionate. What is important is that you think before you post. Sometimes it feels good to rant, but that may not be in your best interest. Remember, everything you post will affect your brand and your narrative for better or worse—so post mindfully!

Stick to Your Narrative

Defining your narrative is one thing, but sticking to it is another. It takes extreme discipline to stick to your narrative. This is especially true when internet trolls try to bait you into an argument. If your goal is to present an aura of safety and refuge from the stress of day-to-day life, then engaging in a debate with somebody who insults you on Facebook or sends you a nasty private message on Twitter is not going to further your goal.

Emotions can be very strong, and that is why I have a policy of never posting anything when I'm in a heightened emotional state. If there is anything remotely questionable about something I'm going to post, I run it by a friend or colleague to get their opinion first. So many people treat social media like a playground for the id—a place we can say and do anything that comes to mind without consequence. But the truth is that everything we say and do has consequences. Once you establish your narrative, stick to it. Don't be baited into going off script.

Sticking to your narrative doesn't mean creating a false narrative. It simply means selectively choosing to post and respond in ways that highlight and underscore the qualities you want to project into the world.

Beware of Trolls

Recently, a woman commented on one of my posts. She felt the need to tell me just how big an idiot I was. She didn't post anything of substance; she just called me names. My initial impulse was to respond in kind. I even started composing a response. It was then that I caught myself. I realize that she had pushed my buttons, and I was preparing to react. Thankfully, I realized this in time and posted a thoughtful response instead. I thanked her for taking the time to write, and that I appreciated her point of view— even if I did not share it.

She wrote back with another tirade of insults. But something else happened. People who followed me on social media began to chime in. They came to my defense. She ultimately gave up.

A few really important things happened though. First, by not taking the bait and not engaging in a pointless insult war, I was able to maintain a narrative of being a yoga teacher who could maintain his calm. Had I responded with insults, I would've taken away from that narrative and lent credence to her grievances. The second thing that happened was that people who felt a connection with me, through my books or classes, felt the need to stand with me. Had I responded to her in kind, they would've felt agitated and frustrated, and may have started to avoid me and my work.

The internet is infested with trolls—people who insult and argue simply because they can. On the internet, anonymity allows people to say and do things that would be completely socially unacceptable in the real world. Sadly, many people take advantage of this, and you will no doubt be the target of trolls from time to time.

It is easy to get your feelings hurt or worse, to respond with the same acrimony that was hurled your way. Mean-spirited comments by trolls can make you want to fold up your laptop, put away your phone and do away with social media altogether. Trolls can also bring out the worst in you. They don't appeal to your better angels, and they can feed your demons if you're not careful. All the hard work that you have put into developing a brand can be destroyed overnight if you give into the trolls.

A reporter friend of mine is Jewish, and his last name reflects that. He works hard to adhere to journalistic standards and ethics to get the facts right and report honestly. In spite of this, his Twitter feed is filled with hateful anti-Semitic messages. He confided in me once that he was almost always tempted to engage with these hatemongers. But the few times that he gave into this temptation did not go well. He never changed anyone's mind or got them to apologize. He simply wasted a lot of his time, diminished his own brand, and encouraged more hateful behavior by other trolls.

It can take a saint-like level of self-awareness and compassion not to respond. I'm not promising it will be easy, but if you are clear about the person you want to be, the narrative you want to weave, and the brand you want to create, you will find it gets much easier. Arguing with trolls will only destroy your brand, zap your energy and encourage their toxic behavior.

Outsource with Fiverr

While much of your brand is based on who you are as a person,teacher, and healer, some things will help to underscore or distract from that brand. The colors, fonts, logos, and other details associated with your brand generate feelings in people. You want these feelings to be consistent with the brand you are trying to create. If you are not naturally gifted in web design, graphic design, photo editing, and so on, I recommend you check out Fiverr. There are thousands of professionals all over the world who are available to help you create quality branding assets that will make you stand out in the crowd.

Design Like a Pro with Canva

If you have some moderate skills but simply need a little help coming up with cool designs, I recommend Canva. With this online service, you can create graphics for all your social media accounts with easy-to-use templates, a vast library of stock photos, and an intuitive interface. Best of all, you can create designs that represent you and then export them with the unique dimensions needed for each social media channel.

Become Inspirational

Chances are people will not be coming to your social media channels to engage with you in the ways they would in the real world. If you are a massage therapist, you can't give them a bodywork session through Twitter, at least not yet. And if you are a yoga teacher, you can't really teach a yoga class through Instagram, though there is an emerging market of online yoga and exercise classes. The reason people will engage with you on social media and want to follow you is for inspiration.

If all people wanted was a parrot to guide them through a yoga class, they would simply by a yoga video. If all they wanted was to have their muscles kneaded into compliance, they would buy a massage chair from Sharper Image. People come to teachers and healers not simply for their skills but for inspiration. A good teacher and healer creates a space that makes people feel safe, inspired, and excited to take steps toward greater healing and personal growth.

People will not follow or engage with a social media feed to read announcements about your business. They will tune into your feed and follow you because you inspire them. You have a story, but that story should be inspirational. Did you lose a lot of weight? Did you overcome a personal challenge? Were you able to quit smoking or recover from a difficult divorce? All of these things make you an inspirational figure, and for people who are dealing with similar issues, it is this that will draw them to you more than anything else.

Some of this inspiration can come from your personal story, but it can also originate from elsewhere as well—perhaps a video that inspires your audience, a powerful quote, or a story about someone overcoming a challenge. Even though these things may have been created by someone else, the fact that you post them inspires the people who follow you. They will in turn associate you with being a source of inspiration.

Engage with Trending Posts

We will talk about trending and what makes it happen in a later chapter, but for the moment know that topics and posts trend on all social media platforms. Sometimes trending topics are tethered to real world events, such as an earthquake, a hurricane, or other tragedy that everybody is posting about. At other times, trending posts may be a video that makes people laugh, cry, or get angry, but whatever it is, a lot of people are talking about it and sharing it.

Ideally you want to create something original that begins to trend, but that's not easy to do. If you can find topics that are trending that are somehow connected to you and your brand, you can forward them, repost them, or better yet comment on them. When you do this, it puts you directly in the line of sight of people who are likely to identify with your brand and your message.

This doesn't mean you shouldn't try to create your own trending content, but you don't need to create everything you post. Keep an eye on Twitter and look for the things that people are talking about. There's a good chance it will trend on all the other social media platforms as well. Your job is to figure out how that topic dovetails with your work and then connect those dots for the people that follow you.

A Picture Tells. . .

Whenever possible, share something with a photo, graphic, or video. The statistics on sharing are clear. When you share something with a visual image of some kind, it gets people's attention. We'll go into more detail on this later, but for the moment know that what you share to create your brand needs a visual component. You can use stock photos, your own personal photos, videos that you create, or videos others have created on sites like YouTube—whatever you like. If you do not have decent visuals, you will basically be invisible, and that is not the brand you want to create.

A video of you doing a chiropractic adjustment demonstration, a photo of you compassionately listening to a psychotherapy client, or a cool image of you teaching at a benefit for cancer research will go a long way to define your brand and further your narrative. You could write a 40-page book with perfect grammar, and it wouldn't have near the impact of sharing a single image on social media. The images you share are the best way to develop and solidify your brand and narrative. Stock photo websites are great places to get professional photos. Envato has a decent selection and is typically much cheaper than other services.

Share, but Don't Overshare!

Part of the reason people will trust you and choose to come to you as a teacher or healer is because they will feel an emotional connection to you. Part of the way you achieve a loyal following on social media is through sharing. Sharing your strengths and weaknesses in a way that inspires people to reach further and live from a posture of hope rather than fear builds the trust and connection you want. Oversharing, however, can be toxic. It can destroy everything you've worked for. The truth is, not everybody cares what you had for breakfast, that your spouse got you a piece of jewelry for your birthday, or that your child threw up all night.

Personal details should be offered with thoughtfulness and care and should further your brand narrative. There's nothing wrong with sharing a story about your child or mentioning a particularly nutritious meal that might inspire your followers to eat more healthily themselves. It might even be worthwhile to note that it's your anniversary and you attribute the love you feel in large part to your meditation practice. But people don't need every detail of your life. They don't want every detail of your life. If you overshare, you will drive people away! Don't be afraid of sharing personal details, but do so in a very judicious way.

Chapter Three:

Alligator Rhythm

Have you ever wondered why things trend the way they do? Have you over wondered why certain photos pop up on your Instagram feed, why certain Facebook posts go viral, why certain posts get shared and liked on Twitter enough to make them trend? If you've ever wondered this, you are not alone. There is an entire industry of people trying to figure out how to crack the code. The goal of all social media marketing is to get people to engage with content, ideally in a way that gets that content in front of new eyeballs well beyond existing circles of influence.

Every social media platform has an algorithm, or as I like to call it, an alligator rhythm. This determines, for better or worse, if a post should be shown to a user as they scroll through Facebook, Twitter, etc. With millions upon millions of posts to social media everyday, it would be impossible for one person to read every post in their feed. Therefore, companies like Facebook, Twitter, and Instagram create a computer algorithm that determines what's most interesting and engaging based on how people are interacting with it.

No one knows for sure what each company's algorithm is. It is like the secret recipe for Diet Coke. But there are some things we know for sure. The backbone of all social media, and the algorithms that drive those platforms, is knowing how users engage in posted content. In short, the more likes, shares, and comments a post gets, the more that social media platform is going to boost its viewership. Of course, the more a post gets boosted by the algorithm, the more likely it will get additional shares, comments, and reposts. Such a post is then said to have gone viral.

The question then becomes, how do we get people to like, share, and repost? If you can figure that out, there is a good chance you can get the content you post to trend or go viral!

Putting the Social Back in Social Media

Social media is first and foremost *social*. I know that sounds like an obvious thing to state, but a shocking number of people don't get this most fundamental principle. Imagine how popular you would be if you went to a cocktail party and, instead of sharing things that emotionally engaged people around you, you simply repeated announcements about your work. Imagine also that you did all the talking and never listened to anyone else's stories or commented on what they shared. Imagine going to that party and acting as if you were the only person in the room. You would probably be labeled a narcissist, people would avoid you, and you probably wouldn't get invited to many more cocktail parties in the future. The reason: your behavior would be completely antisocial.

In the hit TV show *The Office*, there was a minor character named Bob Vance. Any time he was talking to another character, he stuffed a business card in their hand and said, "Bob Vance, refrigerator sales." It was painfully awkward to watch. His goal was to get people to buy refrigerators from him, but he usually only succeeded in alienating everyone around him. This is how so many people approach social media. They post announcements about the work they do, but they don't engage with people in their network. This lack of engagement is the kiss of death. It is the social media equivalent of being a narcissist at a cocktail party.

If you want to succeed in social media, you have to be social. It is a conversation of give and take. It is about emotionally connecting with people as much as, if not more than, intellectually connecting with them. Making announcements and sales pitches about your work has its place, but only when it is surrounded by something that feels genuinely social, emotionally connected, and respectful of others.

So, how do we do this? How do we get people to connect with us on a social and emotional level through social media? Most people know what this looks like in the real world, but how do we do it through a mobile phone, computer, or tablet? There are various models for doing this, but I like the Rule of Four.

What is an Algorithm?

Before we get into the Rule of Four, let's take a moment to consider the algorithm conundrum. While we may not know the exact ingredients in each social network secret sauce, we do know this: all of the algorithms are based on engagement. The more people engage with things you post, the more likely your posts are to rise to the top. Twitter does this in a very simple and straightforward way. The more people who like, retweet, and comment on a post, the more likely it is to trend. Twitter also makes great use of the hashtag, which we will cover in greater detail soon. For the moment, just think of hashtags like keywords.

On the other hand, Facebook uses an algorithm called EdgeRank. Like Twitter, EdgeRank, is based on engagement, but it also takes into account the people in your network, the types of things you already follow, and a whole bunch of other details about your history with Facebook and your personal profile. Facebook has become surprisingly good at showing people the content with which they are most likely to engage.

Other social networks have their own secret sauce, but all of them are based on engagement. The question then becomes how to get people to engage with our content. Try this experiment. Log into one of your social media platforms and look back at your history. Notice the things you shared and liked and commented on over the past month or year. You will likely see a similar pattern.

The things you shared likely made you feel something. Maybe it was a funny video that made you laugh. Maybe it was a news article about political corruption that made you angry. Or maybe it was something that inspired you. Whatever it was, you most certainly felt something when you decided to click the little heart icon, share the post, or comment on the post.

One thing you will not see much of is the sharing and liking of blatant advertisements. People are simply not motivated to engage with an overt sales pitch. This principle is true even if users genuinely like the service or product. This presents a problem because our goal is obviously to promote the work we do. So, if we can't get people to share, like, and comment on the work we do, no one is going to notice, and we will have wasted our time.

Ironically, this also presents an amazing opportunity. As teachers and healers, we are in the business of emotionally engaging with the people we serve. People don't seek out teachers and healers for purely intellectual reasons. They almost always seek out teachers and healers with whom they feel an emotional connection, albeit an often unconscious one. Therefore, your goal should not be marketing a specific event, class, or service. Your goal should should be to get your brand to trend. This means developing an emotional connection and bond with people who follow you or are likely to appreciate your work so that when you do announce something, they will be interested.

Boosting Your Rank with the Rule of Four

The rule of four is quite simple. It basically states that your posts should be divided into four categories.
1. Emotion
2. Inspiration
3. Education
4. Call to Action

Let's look at each of these in turn.

Emotion

The first type of post is the emotional post. Emotional posts are the most likely to be shared, commented on, and liked. One may be a funny video, a witty commentary, or something that makes people cry, get angry, or feel frustrated. The emotion is really irrelevant. It just needs to make them feel something. If you don't believe me, ask

Donald Trump. Donald Trump is best known for his incendiary tweets. People either love him or hate the things he posts to Twitter, but almost everyone feels something. In those strong feelings that he evokes, people react. They feel almost compulsively drawn to comment on what he said, or share what he said, or talk about what he said around the water cooler at work. Whether or not you voted for Donald Trump is not the point. The point is he makes people feel something, and the result is a Twitter feed that is overflowing with trending content.

No, I am not suggesting that you post incendiary things to social media just to get attention. Donald Trump has created a brand for himself that you probably wouldn't want if you're going to brand yourself as a teacher or healer. But, if you can get people to feel something, especially stronger emotions, then they will engage with the content you post.

A few years ago, AARP contacted me. They were doing a series of videos about yoga and America, and they wanted to interview me. When I spoke with them on the phone, I suggested that they make the piece, not about me, but about an inspirational student of mine. His name is Charles, and he still comes to yoga nearly every Tuesday night in a wheelchair. They loved the idea and made a short film about him. They interviewed me and other relevant people, but the focus was on how yoga had helped him come home to his body. The video is very emotional, and very few people can watch it without having their eyes filled with tears. It also went viral, with thousands of people around the world seeing it on YouTube and other social media platforms. You can watch "This is How I Roll" on YouTube.

A talking head video of me telling people how great yoga is is boring. No one wants to watch that. More importantly, no one would want to share it. But a story that moves people to tears and gives hope to people who are struggling with their own body limitations grabs us and demands that we tell others to check it out. Your emotional post should have this quality. You're not trying to tell somebody something—you're trying to help people feel something. At least 25% of your posts should have this quality.

Motivation

The second type of post is the motivational post. There can be some overlap of course—a motivational story can also be very emotional—but a motivational post inspires people to reach higher. It reminds them that they can overcome the obstacles in their lives. It reminds them that they can do it and allows them to feel like they have a cheerleader in you. We all need someone to remind us of our strength and our capacity for healing and growth. We all need to feel like success is possible. It is not enough to simply say this to someone. We have to inspire this from deep within, and various kinds of social media posts can achieve this.

A few years ago, when I hit middle age and my metabolism shifted, I started to put on a few extra pounds. There was a part of me that wanted to simply accept that I was getting old and that this is what old looked like. I then saw a YouTube video of a young man who was significantly overweight. He was addicted to video games and lived on junk food. But one day something snapped, and he decided to make a change. The video then showed his daily routine and it was like a video diary of his progress. For one month, he ate healthy, clean food and did an intense workout everyday. By the end of the month, his body was ripped and lean.

I added this video to my favorites on YouTube, and each day I would watch that video before breakfast. It was a three minute reminder that I could eat well, exercise, and achieve my fitness and health goals. It kept me on track, and it helped me develop strong positive habits that would help me navigate my changing middle-aged body in a way that made me look forward to the second half of life rather than dreading it.

Motivational content is essential. It is particularly useful for us as teachers and healers. It is no surprise that people resist things that are good for them. Like children who turn their noses up to broccoli, our students and clients will find every excuse in the book to avoid the healthy choice. But motivating them on social media is a great way to keep them regular. It is also a great way to get them to share motivational content with others, thus boosting your showing on social media. About 25% of your posts should have a motivational component to them.

Educate

The third type of post is the educational post. Educational posts appeal to the brain. I like to post a lot of scientific studies on the effectiveness of yoga, but you can post educational content that is more suited to the work you do as well. When you come across articles, videos, and other content that will educate your students and clients, be sure to post it. The first two types of posts, emotional and motivational, speak largely to the heart. The educational post speaks to the brain. It reinforces what the previous two types of post set in motion. For example, your personal trainer might want to post a video of someone who lost a lot of weight and got to excellent shape through weight training and mindful dieting. Likewise, you may also want to emotionally engage with potential and existing clients by sharing something about your own struggles and how you overcame them. But you can also take some time to educate them, maybe by sharing a healthy recipe or a new study about the importance of cardiovascular exercise and heart health. The first two types of posts grab people's attention, while the educational post validates what people feel.

Call to Action (CTA)

The final type of post is the call to action. It is here that you post steps that you would like your clients or students to take. This can be as simple as visiting your website or getting on your mailing list. Maybe it involves getting them to try a session with you or take one of your classes. Maybe you want them to buy your book or subscribe to your podcast. As a general rule, you want your call to action to be small and easy to execute. This doesn't mean you can't have larger calls to action, such as asking people to register for a retreat or buy a package of 10 treatments, but you will find more success if you have smaller action items which then lead to bigger ones. Your call to action items should never be more than 25% of your posts. I would argue that keeping it even lower is advisable. Constant calls to action drive people away, but the right number gets people engaged and makes them dedicated customers.

Share Unto Others

Imagine if your best friend asked you for favors all the time but never did anything for you in return. How long do you think that person would be your friend? How long would it be before you got sick of them always calling and wanting something without ever reciprocating? Social media is exactly the same. Not only will the people who follow you on social media not appreciate a one-sided relationship, the algorithms that power almost every social network will punish you for it.

So many people make the mistake of thinking all they need to do to be successful in social media is post announcements about what they're doing. If they have a workshop, post it. If they're running a special on bodywork packages, post it. Often these people never stop to wonder why nobody is sharing or clicking those posts or why social media isn't putting them on people's radar.

Everyone knows the Golden Rule: "Do unto others as you would have them do unto you." It's a great way to live your life. But when it comes to social media, the Golden Rule is "share unto others." The more you comment, repost, like, and mention others' posts, the more likely you are to get traction on social media. Every platform will evaluate this differently, but every platform needs you to share existing content on that platform.

If you're on Twitter, retweet an inspirational post. If you're on Facebook, be sure to tag someone who wrote an article that you're forwarding. If a fellow chiropractor writes an amazing article about the sacroiliac joint, like it or, better yet, repost it. It can be tempting to see others as the competition and think that the only way we can get ahead is by only promoting our own interests. But sharing and mentioning content by others—especially content that is relevant to your audience—is the best way to get the algorithms to notice you and bump you to the top of the heap. It's also good karma!

Cross-Link Your Channels

If you're reading this book, you're probably pretty serious about social media. You want to get good at it, so you're probably choosing a few channels that are well suited to your unique business and your personality. While I don't recommend having more than four social media platforms to manage, having several is not a bad idea. Cross-linking them is a great way to drive traffic to various posts.

For example, if you write a longer post on Facebook, you can mention it on Twitter. You can then provide a link where people can read the longer post and hopefully start following you on Facebook as well. Rather than simply posting a picture to Twitter, maybe you simply link to that photo on Instagram. You can also cross-link in the profile itself for most social media networks. Cross-linking is a great way for people to find you, follow you, and discover the great content you're sharing on various platforms.

Mention Influencers

Nothing will make a post gain traction like mentioning somebody who has a following. There are a number of influencers out there. Some are household names. Some are only known in smaller circles, such as within the yoga community or the bodywork community. Some are not people at all.

Magazines, blogs, YouTube channels, podcasts, and many other venues have a presence on social media. If you're going to post something that you find in one of these venues, be sure to mention them. Not only will they be alerted to the fact that you posted their content, many of their followers will become aware of your posts as well. This is a great way to get like-minded people to follow your social media feeds.

You can also take note of well-known people who have benefited from work similar to what you offer. If you read an article about a famous football player who was able to play the entire season because of deep tissue massage, that is a great thing for any massage therapist to post, and you can mention that player to ensure even more people see it.

The more you mention prominent people and influencers in your post, the more likely that post will be seen by the right people. It will also help potential students and clients connect the dots between the important work you are doing and their unique needs. Because that football player managed his injury with deep tissue massage, maybe they can too. By sharing that post, they'll know who to call.

Jump on a Trend

Social media loves a trend. All of a sudden, everybody will be posting about something happening in the world of entertainment, sports, politics, or the world, creating a flurry of tweets, Facebook posts, or pictures on Instagram across the internet about the topic.

I don't claim to know what makes some things trend and why other things don't, but I do know that connecting a trend to your work is like hitting the jackpot. For example, the wildly popular TV show *Game of Thrones* is sure to trend when a new episode is released. If you know that one of the actors used yogurt to prepare for a particular scene or simply to stay in shape while on the set, you can mention that and even link to an article. Be sure to tag the TV show as well as the actor so that people who follow that TV show or that actor are more likely to see the article you posted. Even though the TV show and the article and the actor have nothing to do with yoga per se, it's a great way to get your work on the radar of hundreds or even thousands of potential followers and customers.

There is one word of caution, however. Don't be gratuitous. Some things trend because they are tragic. A school shooting, a massive earthquake, a celebrity disclosing a cancer diagnosis. Stories like these are likely to trend, and it's perfectly fine to mention them. But be very careful that you don't come off as opportunistic and insensitive. If you're going to post something about a tragedy, make sure you do it in a way that is tactful, ethical, and respectful of the people involved.

Curate Engaging Content
There are millions of videos, articles, scientific studies, infographics, and photos on the internet. If you know where to look, you can find some amazing content to post to social media. This content can entertain, inform, emotionally stimulate, and otherwise move your students and clients. It's also likely to get people to share and repost. The best part is you are helping the creator of that content share their work while keeping people engaged.

A quick search of YouTube will probably provide you with hundreds of inspiring and educational videos that are perfect for posting. A Google News Alert will let you know when topics of interest are in the news. Following some really great blogs that focus on topics of interest to your readers and followers will help you get even more content. In another chapter, we will talk about how you can schedule this content for distribution so that you don't go crazy, but for the moment, start hunting for content that you can link to and share.

Hunt Where the Zebras Graze

Social media is a wild, wild jungle. You can find some of the most inspiring content and people, and you can bump into some of the most hateful individuals and content. The good news is that there are places you can go to find people interested in your work. You can join and post to Facebook groups that focus on topics related to your work. You can find Twitter hashtags that relate to your work. There are entire YouTube channels dedicated to bringing together like-minded people.

It can be very disappointing to work hard on a social media post to have no one like, view, or share it. But if you write something particularly insightful and impressive, or even if you want to post something that you curated, there are probably platforms within each social network where interested people are congregating. If one doesn't exist already, there's probably a mechanism for you to create your own.

Chapter Four:

Engagement

In my book, _The Yogi Entrepreneur: A Guide to Earning a Mindful Living Through Yoga_, I have a section called "Just Because You Can Doesn't Mean You Should." The basic gist of the concept is that more does not always equal better. A similar concept exists within social media. Posting a lot of garbage to social media doesn't make your feed more interesting. Only posting _engaging_ content will keep people coming back and will increase the chances that the algorithms driving each platform will propel you to the top of the heap.

If you think of friendships or business relationships in the real world, there is always a give-and-take. They are not simply one-sided. When a relationship becomes one-sided, it quickly ends. In order for me to enjoy your company and benefit from a friendship with you, I need to engage with you. Perhaps you tell me a joke and I laugh. Or perhaps you share something vulnerable, so I give you a hug. There is a natural give-and-take to every relationship. And this is true of social media relationships as well.

From an algorithmic point of view, engagement is any time someone interacts with something you post. If you post a cute video of a cat chasing a string, people can interact with it if they so choose. Maybe one person likes the post. Another person may comment on the post. Someone else might like it so much that they repost the video. All of this is engagement.

The Secret to Engagement

As we discussed above, boring announcements and sales pitches are not very engaging. The things that get people to engage are emotional, inspiring, and educational. If you want someone to engage with your social media posts, you need to appeal to the heart more than the head. You need to make them laugh, cry, ball their fists in anger, feel like they can improve the quality of their lives or make a difference in the world.

Consider these two tweets and tell me which one you would be more likely to engage.

> Yoga Class with Darren Tuesday night at 6:15 p.m. Learn More: www.darrenmain.com

> One year ago today, I started teaching a class on Tuesday nights. What started off as three people has grown to over 30 people every week! A big thank you to all the students who made this class such a special part of my week. Please help me celebrate my one year anniversary this Tuesday! Learn More: www.darrenmain.com

The first tweet above is flat, boring, and makes few people care about it. The second tweet announces the exact same thing but gets people to feel something about the class. If they've already attended the class, they will feel a sense of pride and ownership because they helped create something special. If they haven't yet attended the class, they probably feel like they've been missing out on something really awesome and will be more likely to give it a shot. Regardless, people reading the second post are far more likely to engage with it. One person may forward it to a friend, another person may click on the link, and a third person might click the heart button. There is also a good chance people will post congratulatory notes and messages.

All of this is engagement, and the algorithms that power social networks give weight to that engagement. It is unlikely that the first tweet would see the light of day, but the second one has a good chance of trending, at least in my community. Getting your post to trend within the right community is exactly what you want.

Choose a Post Schedule

Consistency is essential to engagement. Imagine if you had a friend who only called you sporadically. You'd never know when a call might happen or why they'd be calling. That friend would just sort of show up in your life and then disappear again. It would be very difficult to develop a deep and meaningful connection with that person. The same is true of social media. Remember, the fundamental aspect of social media is the word *social*. It is all about relationships. The consistency with which you post will determine the depth of those relationships as well as the quality and nature of those relationships.

This can be incredibly challenging because it means showing up consistently on social media platforms. This is probably why so many people fail so spectacularly with social media. The idea of having to show up everyday and post clever and insightful things feels overwhelming, so many people simply don't do it at all. Trust me, I feel your pain.

Luckily for both of us, there is a solution that will save you hours of time while improving the consistency with which you post. But before we talk about solutions, let's define what we need. For each teacher and healer the answer will be a bit different, so taking a moment to be honest with yourself about who you are as a person, the level of commitment you're willing to make, and the needs of the people you serve will serve you well.

If we compare consistency in social media with that of parenting, I think you can understand little more about what you need to consider to be successful in your online presence. If a parent is completely absent, that is not good. Children need consistency from their parents, but being a helicopter parent is not good either. In good parenting, we need to strike the right balance between being consistent and predictable while giving children enough space to breathe, develop healthy boundaries, and discover the world for themselves.

The same is true for how we should engage with our social media community. If you never show up, or show up in fits and starts only to disappear for weeks at a time, you will not likely develop a following. Likewise, if you post 50 times a day, people will get annoyed. People want to be inspired and encouraged by their teachers and healers, not suffocated!

As a general rule, one or two posts a day is a good rule of thumb. Unless there is a major reason to do so, I would not post more than three times per day. And unless there is an earth shattering reason not to post, I would definitely post something at least once per day to make sure you stay on people's radar.

Timing is also important. For most teachers and healers, their target audience will be local, so try to post at times when locals are likely to see your post. Many people are having their breakfast and checking social media at around 7 a.m. It is also likely they will be engaging with social media at lunch and then in the evening as they unwind for the day.

You also want to consider the four types of posts discussed above. Ideally there is a mix of them. Some people have a hard rule about this though. They post on a very strict schedule, but I personally take a more laid-back approach. I try to be aware of posting a variety of things, making sure not to stack a day or even a week with too many emotional or educational posts. I definitely try to be mindful not to make too many call to action posts back to back.

Trial and error will help you figure out when to post each type of engagement, but starting with the general schedule is a good idea until you discern the needs of your community and what they respond to most often. You can also take note of the time of day when your community interacts the most. Remember, there is no one-size-fits-all when it comes to social media. Try to get a feel for your community and do your best to keep them engaged.

Use a Scheduling Service

As I promised above, there is a solution to make all of this relatively pain free and effortless. The solution is to use a scheduling service such as Buffer or HootSuite. There are other services as well, but these two are the most popular. Each service has features that the other does not, so you'll want to investigate both to see which one is a better fit for you, but they both fill roughly the same role at the end of the day.

Once you sign up for a service, you can give that service access to your various social media channels. Both services cover the big ones, but if you have a passion for lesser-known social media outlets, you will definitely want to make sure the service you choose is compatible with the social media platforms you want to use.

Once you have linked your social media accounts with the scheduling service, you can start posting to all of the channels at once or just the channels you choose for a given post. There are several convenient ways to schedule your posts.

Send Now: Once you compose a post, you can send it immediately. It will show up on all of your social media channels within minutes. This is akin to logging into Facebook or Twitter, writing a post, and hitting send. While it is convenient to post to all of your platforms at once, this is not the most powerful use of the service. It is useful, however, if you want to do a last minute or time sensitive post.

Schedule

You can also compose a post, choose where to post it, and then schedule when the post will go live. This is particularly helpful if you have time sensitive announcements that will take place in the future. Perhaps you are running a Valentine's Day sale that begins on February 1. Rather than reminding followers of this yourself on the morning of February 1, you can simply compose a post a week in advance and schedule its release for the appropriate date and time. I use this feature all the time to remind people of early bird specials coming to a close, to wish people a happy holiday, or to remind people of my monthly meditation group. The best part is that once you have scheduled these posts, you can forget about them altogether, trusting that they will be delivered at the perfect moment to alert your followers of whatever is going on.

Queue the Post

For a large number of your posts, the exact day and time is not all that relevant. Perhaps you see an article in the *New York Times* about the benefits of meditation for anxiety. This is a perfect article to post if you are a meditation instructor since it educates your followers about the benefits of taking one of your classes. However, this kind of content doesn't need to be sent immediately or at a specific time in the future. This is a perfect item to add to your queue.

Your queue is a running list of posts that will be delivered in order at a specific time each day. You can choose the posting schedule that works best for you. Perhaps you want a message posted every morning at 7 a.m. and another one posted every afternoon at 4 p.m. Services like Buffer and Hootsuite will simply post at those times as long as you have a message waiting to go live. You can rearrange your queue at any time, making it easy to bump a new article you found to the top of the queue.

In theory, you could take an hour once a month and load up your queue with dozens of posts. These could include content that you created yourself, such as a blog post on your website or video you made for YouTube, or they could be curated content such as the *New York Times* article mentioned above.

Each scheduling platform will have a slightly different user interface for managing the queue, but the principle for them all is basically the same: you load up your queue in the service host and set a time for content to go live. Sprinkled into that mix will be posts that you schedule or send immediately. Using one of these services will help keep your audience fully engaged, and you won't have to think about your social media networks more than a few times a month.

Explore Peak Times

When is the right time to post? This is a question that has been debated by hundreds and perhaps thousands of social media marketing professionals. Countless hours of research have gone into determining the best time to post.

There are several ways to approach this question. Personally, I take a much more laid-back approach. I did a very unscientific survey of my posts' engagement at different times of the day. I realized that many of my followers were more likely to click at about 8:35 in the morning. Of course, 8:35 a.m. in San Francisco is not the ideal time in Tokyo. I also realized that mid-afternoon posts around 4:30 in the afternoon tended to get more traffic and engagement.

Services like Buffer and HootSuite can help you determine the peak times for posting. You can download data about your networks specifically, or you can look at general trends in posting on social media more broadly. These services also offer analytic reporting. You can easily view and compare statistics about various posts. This is a great way to make informed decisions about your posting schedule and about the types of posts your network responds to most favorably.

There so many unknowable factors about posting, but over time you will start to see definite patterns and trends emerging. I would recommend using the suggested times your scheduling service offers to start, but know that your unique audience may not fit neatly into those traditional peak times.

You can also try different times on different networks. The ways people consume posts on Twitter, for example, are significantly different than the ways people consume content on Facebook. The nice thing about a scheduling service like Buffer and HootSuite is that you can pick a schedule for each network you use, allowing you to make identical posts at different predetermined times on different platforms.

Just remember, nothing is set in stone. If a particular posting time doesn't seem to be getting any traction, be sure to mix things up. Notice the trends in the statistics, and you will find the perfect posting schedule for your unique online presence.

Hacks for Engagement

Comment on Hot Topics

One way to increase engagement is to comment on or post about already trending topics. While we need to be careful about not devolving into political debates and agitating half of our following, it can be very useful to comment on things that are happening now.

Perhaps there is a movie that was just released in which the main character gets a massage or goes to a yoga class. Maybe a natural disaster has devastated a community somewhere in the world, prompting you to ask your following to contribute to the Red Cross or another charity.

You can also do fun things that will make people laugh or want to forward your post. Maybe the Oscars are happening, so you could write a post about which movies correspond with various healing modalities. The opportunities are endless. You don't need to do contortions or backflips, just look for natural sequiturs. If something is happening in pop culture or the news, and you can comment on it in a noncontroversial way, do so to get people to forward, comment, and like your post.

Mention Prominent People

There are different ways to mention people on social media. Twitter uses the @ symbol to tag other Twitter users. When you comment on a person or product, Facebook will often automatically tag them in that post. Other social media networks will allow some form of person-to-person tagging as well.

By mentioning prominent people and tagging them in the appropriate way on each network, you will invite all of their followers to check out what you're saying. For example, if I learned that Oprah Winfrey just started a meditation practice, I could post a link to the article and @-mention her by adding the tag @oprah. By adding the simple tag, her 40 million+ members will be alerted to the post. This doesn't mean all 40 million subscribers to her feed will see your post, but even if a small percentage become aware of what you wrote, that is a huge number of eyeballs looking at what you have to say.

Of course you don't have to tag mega-celebrities like Oprah to gain traction. In fact, tagging lesser-known but still prominent people can be even more effective. Perhaps the police chief in your local community attends your qigong class. You could politely ask him to pose in a picture with you. You could then post the picture on Instagram and other social networks and tag him. There is a good chance that many people in your local community will become aware of this photo and consider taking your class.

You can also @-mention prominent people in your field. If you practice sports massage, for example, you could mention an article by a prominent sports massage therapist about knee injuries and tag her. You could also mention some of the athletes with whom she works. This would exponentially increase the reach of the post.

Make Them Laugh, Make Them Cry

If you look back over all of the comments you made on a given social network and consider how often you liked and shared posts, you will definitely notice a trend. The content that made you laugh or smile or brought a tear to your eye is likely the content you engaged with.

If you want engagement, make your followers laugh, smile, or weep. Posting a boring announcement about a new class will likely not get much traction, but posting an inspiring video or something that makes people laugh or smile in a good-natured way will.

People are much more likely to engage in your less emotional content if they get in the habit of liking, sharing, and commenting on your other posts. If the only thing you ever offer is boring sales pitches, good luck with engagement.

Post Photos

If you post text only, the chances are slim that somebody will notice it. However, a post with a photo is 40% more likely to achieve engagement than a post without one. Think about that: the simple act of posting a photo will help you improve engagement by nearly half.

Posting personal photos is ideal. But you can also pull photos from stock photo websites, and many articles you link to will have feature images embedded in them to increase traction. If a photo is not displayed in your post, you might as well not post it at all.

Post Videos

About the only thing that gets more engagement than a photo is a video. Even a short video will increase your chances of engagement. If you're wondering where you can get videos to post, look no further than YouTube. Simply linking to a YouTube video will display that video on your wall or in your feed. A quick search of YouTube will supply you with enough content-relevant videos for a lifetime.

Ask Questions & Use Polls

Asking questions will drive comments. Let's say you're thinking about starting a new Pilates class. You could ask your social media channels which day they prefer. This will give you valuable information about when the class is most likely to succeed, of course, but it will also drive engagement. When you ask a question, people are infinitely more likely to comment, and all of those comments improve your ranking on social media.

Be Edgy Without Being Controversial

Not everyone is good at being edgy. Most people shy away from anything controversial altogether or go way overboard and offend half the people following them. There is a happy medium, however. For example, the issue of gun laws inevitably comes up after every mass shooting. You probably have a strong opinion about the issue, as most people do.

You can certainly make that opinion known, but if you can do it in a way that embraces people with an opposing point of view, you will be able to share your views without alienating half of your followers. At the end of the day, teachers and healers are about holding space. That doesn't always mean forcing your own personal opinion down someone's throat. It does, however, mean challenging people from time to time in a way that is loving and spacious.

Set Google News Alerts

A great place to find awesome content to share on social media is Google. In fact, Google has a service called News Alerts. Rather than going day after day onto Google News and searching for topics your followers might be interested in, you can set up an alert to notify you when an article, blog post, podcast, video, or other type of media is posted. This will give you a steady stream of relevant content to share on social media.

I use a service called Feedly to aggregate all the Google News Alerts and blogs that I follow. This makes reviewing the content much faster, and you can share things directly with Buffer and HootSuite from Feedly. You can use their web browser plugin for your laptop or desktop computer, or you can use their iOS or Android app for your mobile device.

Follow Relevant YouTube Channels

YouTube has changed the way we watch videos. Not only can you watch cute videos of people's cats and babies, you can also find rich content that your social media followers will love. In fact, there are many channels out there that produce weekly or even daily videos that are perfectly suited for various healing and spiritual disciplines.

By following these channels, you will be alerted when new content is released, and you can share that with your audience. Videos are great for keeping people engaged, and since other people are creating such great content, it's easy to do.

The Reddit Gold Mine

If you haven't checked out Reddit, it is a wonderful resource for finding content ripe for sharing. There are parts of Reddit (subreddits) dedicated to just about every topic you can imagine. If you're really into reiki, there's probably a subreddit that will have content just about that topic. If transcendental meditation is your thing, there's probably a subreddit for that as well. If you go on the Reddit website or download their app, you can easily search for topics of interest. You will find a treasure trove of amazing content and you'll probably find some stuff that will make you laugh until you fall off your seat at the same time.

Publish Original Content

Creating your own content is an amazing way to really connect with the people who follow you. Some people produce videos to educate or inspire their audience. Other people write blog posts or have a podcast. Some people do a combination of things.

Chances are one of these content types speaks to you more than others. My advice is to pick one format that you really enjoy and focus on that. You can always add in other types of content that you personally create later. In the beginning, many people try to do everything. They want to write five articles a week for their blog, produce at least two videos a week for their YouTube channel, and have five podcast episodes a week to keep people totally engaged. Inevitably, they get burned out and nothing gets created.

Pick one type of content that you enjoy creating and commit to producing at least one piece of content in that format each week. I would recommend creating a publishing schedule so that you know what's coming up. If you're going to do a series of videos, know what each video will be about, when it will be released, and how it ties into the overall theme of your social networking strategy.

You can also publish your original content on *Huffington Post* or prominent blogs in your field. This helps to brand you as a professional and can drive people to your social media feeds and website.

Learn to Use Analytics

One of the awesome things about most social media platforms is the real-time feedback you can get from your followers. They may or may not comment on the things you post, but you can look at what types of content are most engaging. Facebook, for example, has a robust analytics system. This is a great way to look at the effects of any Facebook ads you choose to run, and it's also a great way to look at the types of posts that are most engaging to your followers.

If you notice that engagement goes considerably up every time you post a video, but goes down when you post an article from a science journal, you have learned some useful information about the types of content that will engage your followers in the future.

SIMPLE Call to Action Requests

At the end of the day, calls to action should be a small percentage of your overall posts, but they are also the most important posts from a business standpoint. After all, the reason you're on social media as a professional is to engage with existing and potentially new customers. If they don't ultimately buy something from you, then what's the point? You may have fun with social media, but (in theory) you're using this as a marketing tool. Therefore, call to action posts are vital to reaching your marketing goals.

Do you want people to sign up for your email list, visit your website, or take a free class? Maybe you want to sell gift certificates for massage sessions on Valentine's Day, or perhaps you want people to come to an introductory workshop on the martial arts program you offer.

All of these are calls to action. You're asking your followers to do something. It can be as simple as clicking a button or dropping their email address in a form, or it can be something more involved, such as getting in the car, driving across town, and taking a yoga class.

Getting people to engage in a call to action is much harder than getting people to engage with a video or an article. In order to have success with call to action posts, you need to remove as much friction as possible between the person and the action you want them to take.

Which of the following two examples would you be most likely to engage with?

- Want a FREE yoga class? Click Here.

- If you'd like to take my class for free, click here, fill out a form with your email address, and I will send you a gift certificate.

The less people have to think about a call to action, the more likely they will engage in that action. In the first post above, you're tickling something in their brain. Almost everybody wants a free yoga class, and all they have to do to get it is click. Before they even know it, they will have clicked the link, dropped in their email address, and downloaded a free class pass. In the second post, people start to think, "Oh my God, I have to fill out a form and give up my email address, and then I get a gift certificate and then. . ."

Keep it short, keep it simple, and people will engage with your call to action requests.

Chapter Five:

Building Your Network

The Chicken or the Twitter Egg

You may already have a social media presence and are reading this book to learn how to achieve more impressive results. Maybe you are brand new to social media and recently created social media accounts. Whatever the case, you are probably facing what I call *the chicken or the Twitter egg conundrum*.

What is a Twitter egg? you might ask. The Twitter egg is the default profile image for new Twitter accounts. It is also a telltale sign that an account is new—or worse, a fake. There are a number of services that will help you identify quality people to follow and avoid the fakes, but let's consider a few high-profile social media celebrities first.

Donald Trump is loved by some and hated by many, but both supporters and non-supporters can agree that Donald Trump is a Twitter sensation. At the time of this writing, he had over 51 million followers. That is a staggering number. There is a catch, however. That number, while impressive, is not an accurate number. According to an October 2017 article in *Newsweek* magazine, nearly half of his followers are fake:

The Daily Dot reported that Twitter analyses of the president's accounts found that about half of his 41.3 million followers rarely tweet or have inactive accounts, and more than a quarter have accounts with no posted tweets as of October.

Now, if you are a fan of Donald Trump, you likely think I'm picking on him because I don't like his politics. But this is not just a Trump thing. Hillary Clinton has a similar issue.

A quick search on Twitter Audit shows that [Trump] has about 19.7 million fake followers and 21.5 million real followers. In comparison, the website says former presidential candidate Hillary Clinton has 9 million real followers and 10 million fake followers.

Both Donald Trump and Hillary Clinton had an agenda—to get more people to vote for them instead of their opponent. But here is a little known fact about American politics: fake Twitter accounts are not allowed to vote! Having millions of bots follow you may stroke your ego, but it doesn't further your cause. Whether you are looking for votes, massage clients or karate students, bots will do nothing to help you achieve your goals.

Worse still, bots create a swamp in which quality content becomes extremely diluted by fake profiles and fake posts. The good news for Trump and Clinton is that half of one million is still 500 thousand. Both have impressive numbers of real people following them. But the fake followers are actually hurting their chances of getting their message out there.

So, how do you get people to follow you if you don't have content, and how do you get your content to trend if you don't have followers? It's a problem to be sure, but in this chapter, we will look at ways to build a following that is targeted and substantial.

TIP

Identifying fake and spam accounts can a full-time job without a little help. Services such as Social Oomph and Manage Filter are great at identifying bogus accounts and allow you to disassociate yourself from them with a few clicks. Both services have a free option, but you can upgrade for more robust tools for a small fee.

Go to the Watering Hole

The goal on Twitter, Facebook, and other platforms is not simply to develop a large number of followers. If you do that, you may just end up with a bunch of fake followers, fake accounts, and spammers. The real goal is to identify your target audience and then invite those specific people to follow you.

Unless you're a nationally recognized teacher or an international lecturer or author, you're probably going to focus on people living in your local community. Furthermore, you're going to want to focus on people who have a specific interest in what you're offering whether directly or indirectly. For example, if you are a meditation teacher, you could target people who are interested in meditation. That is obvious. But you could also target people who are interested in healthy food, other spiritual pursuits, yoga or massage therapy, or other activities complementary to meditation.

Identifying your audience and then going to the places online and in the real world where those people are likely to congregate will help you to build a following that is not only impressive in terms of numbers but effective in reaching the right people.

Hacks for Dramatically Growing Your Network

Cross-link Your Networks

One of the easiest ways to grow your various networks is to cross-link them. In most social media profiles there is a profile option to list your other networks. Your Twitter feed can cross-link with your Facebook feed, and your Facebook feed can cross-link with your Instagram account, and so on.

By cross-linking your various accounts, you will grow each of your platforms more quickly. Some people may find you on Twitter and then also follow you on Facebook for example. This is a simple, quick, and free way to grow your social media presence.

Integrate Your Website with Social Networks

Be sure to use plugins and other tools to help people easily follow you from your website. If you're using a WordPress-based site, this should be fairly easy. Your web developer can help you with this if you're not very tech savvy. The goal is to have anyone who finds your website be able to share blog posts and events on social media and follow you with ease.

Social Proof

Social proof is essential. People are much more likely to follow a person on social media if they already have a following and if people are already talking about them and engaging with their content. This of course can create a chicken and egg conundrum. One way to remedy this is to invite people to post to your social media network or to contact you through Facebook or Twitter rather than traditional email. The more followers you have, the more likely people are to follow you. Some WordPress plugins will allow a count of your followers on various networks. When someone sees a counter with a high number, they're more likely to hit the button to subscribe.

If You Want to Lead, Follow!

Many people start a Twitter or Facebook account and wonder why no one wants to follow them. Of course, they haven't followed anyone themselves, but they think people will come to them just because. One of the best ways to build your following on any platform is to follow other like-minded people. Share their content when appropriate, comment on things people post, and engage with other people as much and as often as you feel comfortable.

If there is a teacher or healer in your community, engage with them. All of their followers will see your name popping up from time to time, and if they like what you post, say, or share, they are more likely to check out your social media feed and even follow you.

Join Facebook groups

Facebook groups exist for every conceivable area of interest. Whether you are interested in massage, Zen meditation, holistic health, vegetarian cooking, or anything else, there is a Facebook group out there. If there isn't an existing Facebook group, you can start one.

By joining Facebook groups and then providing interesting content on that group's wall, you will bring attention to the work you're doing. This makes it easy for people to click through and follow you if they like the things you share with the group. It's a great way to get on the radar of like-minded people and build an amazing network.

Cross Pollinate with Your Email List

While this book isn't about building an email list, there is an opportunity for cross pollination. Many social networks offer features that help your followers quickly subscribe to your email list. The reverse is also true. In your email blasts, be sure to invite people to like your social media channels.

Many services like MailChimp will have this automatically integrated into the emails you send once you set it up. People who follow you through email are much more likely to also follow you on social media platforms.

Invite Direct Messages

When you're teaching or working with a client, you can invite people to direct message you on the platforms you use. This is similar to giving they your email address, but has the added advantage of having then engage with you on social media. A direct message is like an email sent through a social media platform. Whether somebody sends you a Twitter direct message or a Facebook message or contacts you through Instagram, such messages are great ways to put your social media channels on their radar and encourage them to check it out.

One word of caution, however. If you're going to invite people to direct message, you need to be prepared to respond. Nothing is more off-putting than reaching out to somebody with a heartfelt message and then not getting a reply.

Publish Your Feed on Your Website

There are wonderful plugins for WordPress websites that will post things from your various feeds to your website automatically. Whenever you put something on Twitter, Facebook, Instagram, or another social media platform, it will automatically show up on your website. If people reading your website like the posts they see on your site, there is a good chance they will click through and follow you on that platform.

Ask Influencers to Mention You

There are influencers everywhere. Some are prominent in your local community. Others have a national or international presence. Not all will be willing to mention you, but if you write or create something of particular interest to an influencer, make sure they're aware of it. You can even send it to them in a direct message explaining that this article or video you created might be of interest to their followers. Having somebody prominent mention you on social media is one of the best ways to get new and relevant people to check you out and follow you.

Interview Influencers and Co-host Events

Everyone has a circle of influence, though some are larger than others. If you host online events, such as Facebook live conversations, webinars, or interviews with prominent influencers, and then post them to social media, many of their followers will check you out.

When I started my *Inquire Within* podcast and began interviewing authors, teachers, and healers, I saw my social media channels explode with popularity. As soon as I would post an interview from a prominent person, many of their devoted followers would learn about podcast, listen to it, and become aware of me and my social media presence.

Maybe you could host a conversation with a local chiropractor about safe back bending in yoga, or maybe you want to interview a local author about the benefits of massage therapy for cancer patients. There are countless things you can do with influencers that will both honor their work and make others aware of your work.

Mention People

The @-mention is one of the best ways to grow your feed. Whether it's on Facebook, Twitter or another social media platform, when you mention someone else all of the people that follow that person will be alerted to your comments. For example, if you see an article that is relevant to your followers, be sure to post it. But also be sure to give them credit. If you mention the author of the article and any prominent people noted in the article, all of those people's followers will become aware of your post. If you have other relevant content on your wall, they are likely to see it and follow you as well.

Public Thank You

This tip is a simple one, but it couldn't be more important. If professionals in your community send people your way or do things that support you, calling them out on Facebook with the public thank you is a great way to encourage them to do more. Not only does this reward them by bringing awareness to their business, it also builds a deeper connection with them and their network. Whenever you do this public thank you, make sure Facebook's automatic tagging feature kicks in and links the post to their professional page.

Chapter Six:

Pro Hacks for Facebook

In this chapter, we're going to go over some tips and tricks specifically for Facebook. Regardless of which social networks you choose, Facebook will likely be one of them. It is robust and has features that are going to really help you grow your business. Let's dive in to make sure you get the most out of your Facebook experience.

Pay-Per-Click
One of the best features about Facebook is their pay-per-click (PPC) advertising program. PPC is basically a system of targeting specific demographics that you want to reach based on very detailed data points. Facebook then displays your ads for the people who match your specifications. If people click on your ad, you pay a small amount to Facebook. The best part about PPC advertising is you can set your budget, so you never spend more than you can afford.

Let's use an example. Let's say you are leading a retreat for middle-aged women. The retreat is to be held in Costa Rica, and you plan to market your retreat to women in the United States. Advertising would be very, very expensive if you didn't narrow your audience considerably.

Social Media for Teachers and Healers

By using Facebook targeting you can narrow your efforts to the demographics you want to reach. You can set the parameters based on location (the United States), gender (women), age (between 40 and 60), and interest (yoga, spirituality, meditation, and so on).

Honing in on this target audience will ensure your ad appears to people who are likely to be interested in your retreat, and the people who click on it are very likely to be interested in your retreat. When you set up the ad, you can bid on how much you will pay per click. This can be as little as a few cents or into the high-dollar range. You can also set how much you are willing to spend per day. In doing this, you can decide how much reach you want to have and exactly how much you are willing to spend.

You can target ads in smaller geographic areas as well. Perhaps you live in a larger city and want to market your massage business only to people in a specific neighborhood, or maybe you want to target people who go to the yoga studio at which you teach. Those people will often have liked the studio's fan page, and you can use that as a data point.

Facebook PPC is a game changer in your efforts to build your mindful business!

A/B Split Testing

It can be challenging to tell if an ad campaign is working, but a process called A/B split testing can help you determine which version of an ad is yielding the best results. For example, suppose you want to market a holiday gift certificate campaign. You could run several ads that are identical in most ways but change the image you are using. After running both ads for a short period of time, you can compare the results and see which photo is working better.

A/B split testing may seem like a lot of work, but it will help you craft more effective ads and save you a lot of money in the long term. If you really want to hone your A/B split testing skills, there are some great books and Udemy videos that will go into much more detail than is possible in this short book.

Targeted Ads

You may have one thing you want to promote, but you may want to promote it to different types of people. Let's use the holiday gift card example from above. Let's say you want to run your sale for the month of December. The consideration to make is that not everyone celebrates the same holidays. You could easily run the same ad but change the details slightly. You might run an ad targeting people who identify as Jewish and use a photo of a Menorah. You could run the same ad but target people identifying as Christian and us an image of a nativity scene. You could run a third ad targeting people who are atheist, agnostic, or spiritual but not religious and use an image of people ice skating.

In this way you could use the same CTA (buy a gift certificate) but appeal to people who celebrate the holiday season in different ways based on their religious declaration in their Facebook profile. Once New Year's rolls around, you could run a "New Year's Resolution" campaign that targets men and women or different age groups separately.

Facebook Apps

Your cell phone, laptop and tablet have apps, which can be installed to make these devices more functional. Likewise, Facebook offers a robust ecosystem of apps made by both Facebook and third-party developers. These apps add functionality to your Facebook page that will help you build a reputation, deepen your connection to the followers of your page, and invite them to take action. There are far too many apps to list here, but a quick Google search will reveal the most popular ones for small businesses, and there are new ones popping up everyday.

Facebook Events

For study groups, meditation groups, workshops, retreats, or any other type of event, Facebook events are essential. The concept is that you simply plug in the basic information for the event (time, date, location, and so on), post a graphic associated with the event, and provide a text description of what will happen. You can even have a button linked to your preferred registration service like MindBody Online or Eventbrite. Once the event is live on your Facebook event calendar, you have the option of using Facebook PPC to promote the event. You can also link the event to your website if you use WordPress.

Facebook Live

Live streaming is all the rage. You will often see people at political rallies or concerts streaming what is going on. In effect, everyone with a smartphone has the ability to be a reporter. Live streaming your classes, talks, and special events is a great way to generate interest. You can also use services like Zoom to live stream interviews and conversations with other professionals or people of interest.

While live streaming is relatively new when compared to Facebook itself, it is quickly becoming an essential part of the Facebook platform. If you are creative, you can use live stream technology to really boost your visibility.

Call to Action Buttons

You should employ call to action buttons as soon as possible. What do you hope people who like your page will ultimately do? Do you want them to visit your website? Join your email list? View your schedule of classes or book a massage or other session? These are Examples of CTAs, and Facebook allows you to have a button front and center on your professional page. This makes it easy for people to quickly schedule a massage, get more information, or sign up for your email list!

Facebook Groups

Your professional page on Facebook is a way to highlight your work, but there are other ways to get your message out there and support the broader community at the same time. If your work involves a specific issue, you can start a Facebook group for people to congregate online around that issue. For example, I do a lot of work with yoga teachers and healers as a result of my book, *The Yogi Entrepreneur*. I started a companion Facebook group for like-minded people to come together and discuss mindful business practices. This was a great way for me to reach a broader audience and build a sense of community around a specific topic.

Maybe you work with overweight women or focus on issues related to men's health. Perhaps you are reaching out to a non-English-speaking community in your city or are working with kids and their families. There are countless ways for you to become an expert in starting a group where people can get information and connect with others. Connecting others within that target community is a great way to brand yourself and promote the important work you're doing.

Facebook Pixel

Like Google Analytics, Facebook Pixel is an analytics tool that will help you gauge the effectiveness of your Facebook marketing strategy. With Pixel, you can easily track your click rate and see which marketing strategies are working.

The whole system can feel a bit complex, but the process is fairly simple once you set it up. You will need to install a snippet of code into your website so that Pixel can track the traffic to your site from Facebook. Once you do this, Pixel will give you a very granular sense of how people interact with Facebook and your site. You will know how many people are clicking through to your site, how long they're staying on your website, and other important data points that will help you make more informed choices about your marketing campaign.

Chapter Seven:

Pro Hacks for Twitter

Twitter is, of course, the other major social media platform. While it has a lot of similarities to Facebook, it is also very different in some key ways. You can also use Twitter in ways that are uniquely suited to the platform. Let's look at some professional hacks to get the most out of your Twitter presence. The key to success on Twitter is content. If you are not posting quality content that engages your audience, you are unlikely to succeed on the platform.

A Steady Flow

Just as going to the gym once every three weeks will not produce meaningful results, tweeting only on occasion will receive very little engagement, growth in your following, or an increase in business. This is true of other networks as well, but for Twitter in particular, this principle is paramount. Keep the content flowing, or your Twitter feed will soon dry up like a creekbed in a drought.

Mimic Following

Twitter is a social network, and in order to succeed on a social network, you need to keep in mind that the first word in that phrase is *social*. You cannot set up a Twitter feed and expect people to follow you just because you are a great person.

People will want to follow you on Twitter because you have rich content and you follow them first. If you think about going to a cocktail party or a nightclub, and you want to meet lots of interesting people, somebody has to be brave and make the first move. Somebody has take that social risk to introduce themselves and start a conversation.

Likewise, finding relevant people to interact with on Twitter requires you to take the initiative. The easiest way to find relevant people who are likely to be interested in your work is to engage a process called *mimic following*.

Mimic following is simply following the followers of related Twitter feeds. For example, I wrote a book about the business of yoga. My goal was to reach out to people who would be interested in that topic. The obvious place to look was popular Twitter feeds that spoke to the needs of yoga teachers. Feeds like Yoga Journal, Yoga Alliance, and Yoga International were all logical choices, and each of them had thousands of followers.

A high percentage of their followers were likely going to be interested in the work I was doing to support yoga professionals. By following the followers of those popular feeds, I extended a handshake and an introduction to those people.

Some of them turned out to be disinterested or fake profiles, but a good percentage of the people I followed in those networks followed me as well. I formed some amazing connections, and I built my Twitter following very quickly.

Follower/Following Ratio

There are a few cautionary things to be aware of before you use this technique, however. You want to make sure the people you are following are people who are engaging with you. If you follow thousands of accounts and only a handful of people are following you in return, that ratio will set up red flags for both Twitter and services that filter out probable spammers. Your goal should be to have more followers than people you follow. The easiest way to do this is to continually sift through and unfollow the bad apples. There are services that will help you do this. Social Oomph and Manage Filter are two of the more popular ones. They will help you identify good people to follow who post often and are unlikely to be bots. They will also help you find people who are not behaving or engaging with your Twitter feed. Those people who are not good actors can be quickly unfollowed, keeping your ratio in proportion.

Clean House

I set a calendar alert to go through my Twitter feed and clean out any bots or fake accounts once a month. The truth is that while these higher numbers may make you feel good, they will ultimately water down your message and make you stick out as a possible spammer with the various filters online. Keeping your Twitter feed healthy and as free as possible from bots and spammers will make your messaging that much more effective.

Monitor the Trends

There are obvious issues and news bits that will connect with your business. You can set up a Twitter alert for topics associated with your brand of healing or teaching. For instance, you can follow the hashtag for martial arts, karate, yoga, or holistic health. You can follow hashtags that are obviously related to you and your business, but you can also look at general trends. If you see a celebrity is doing a lot of social justice work, and you know that celebrity has a strong meditation practice, you might want to mention that. You can link to an article about the social justice work they're doing, mention that a fellow meditator is out there doing good work in the world, use appropriate hashtags, and @mention them to see if you can get something to trend based on their noteworthy reputation and work. The easiest way to do this is to get a Twitter client such as Twitterrific to help you monitor the Twitter universe for things that may be of interest.

Monitor Hashtags

A hashtag is really just a keyword preceded by the pound sign (#). Anyone can start a hashtag on anything, and anyone can follow any hashtag. Some hashtags are cute and clever and trend for a short time. If a celebrity does something silly or a politician embarrasses themselves, you can be sure that hashtag will be formed almost immediately to bring attention to it. But other hashtags can be more long-lasting. If you do a quick search on Twitter, you can see if there are existing hashtags for the work you do. If one doesn't exist, you can start one.

By using prominent hashtags, people who are interested in a specific subject are likely to see the things you post. For example, if I write an article about yoga and its benefits for HIV patients, I can hashtag that post with a #HIV and #yoga. In this way, anyone interested in those two subjects is likely to see it. This greatly extends my reach well beyond my own circle of influence, and it helps me target the exact people I want reading my article. You can do the same with almost anything you're doing. The reach a hashtag can give your post is exponentially greater than using no hashtag at all.

Cast a Retweet Spell

If you spend any time on Twitter, you have no doubt come across the letters 'RT', the acronym for retweet. If you ask somebody to retweet a post, there is a huge increase in the number of people who will do it. I have found that doing this with every Twitter post is counterproductive, but if there is something really important to get out there, putting the phrase "please RT" in the body of the tweet will boost the number of retweets.

Chapter Eight:

Pro Hacks for Instagram

Instagram is a standalone platform owned by Facebook that focuses on the visual. You can share images and videos from your life and work to create a visual narrative and brand. Best of all, your students and clients can tag you in photos, helping to build buzz about your work. Let's look at a few hacks to make your Instagram feed look professional.

Telling Stories

Instagram should be so much more than a link to your camera roll. You should be telling a story about your life or your work through photos, videos, and text. Avoid thinking about it as individual photos and start to think of it as a story arc.

For example, if I wanted to use Instagram to promote this book, I might post a photo of me at a local cafe writing, a selfie of me speaking at a conference about social media, or an image of the new cover. Once the book is released, I could post a video of me unboxing my first shipment of books hot off the press and photos or selfies with people who come to lectures and book signings.

Each post should contribute to a story arc for followers to engage in a visual narrative. The arc of this narrative can be years long or shorter in duration. I tend to think of posts like chapters in a novel. While the entire novel tells a longer narrative, the chapters tell shorter narratives that contribute to the whole.

For example, your greater narrative may be one about a struggle with obesity and food addiction that was ultimately overcome through Overeaters Anonymous, gentle yoga, and daily meditation. Now that you are a yoga teacher, your personal journey can inspire others. This story can be told through images and videos in a very dramatic way. Perhaps you post photos of yourself as a child eating candy, with a caption explaining that your mother would often give you sugar to calm you down when you were upset. You could also post before and after photos of how your body changed once you started your journey. You could also post a photo of a delicious yet healthy meal you created along with a recipe.

In addition to the the long arc of your visual narrative, you may also want to highlight specific "plot points." For example, if you led a retreat for women about having a healthy body image, you could, with permission, post photos from the retreat that tell the visual story of how the women who attended were able to tap into their power and reframe their narratives about their bodies. This not only tells the story of the retreat, but also contributes to your broader narrative.

Finally, you could invite your students to tag you in their posts. When someone takes your yoga class and has success in changing their relationship with food and their body, a before and after photo is a powerful testimonial that is sure to inspire other students and those who have not yet experienced your class.

Aesthetics Set the Mood

Will the photos and videos you post be abstract, selfies, black and white or in color? Will they be action shots, head shots, or images of objects? Will the lighting be soft or dramatic? Will they be professional or intentionally candid shots from your smartphone? The subject of a photo or video is only part of the image. The aesthetic of the image or video creates a mood or tone. There is no right or wrong answer, but the types of images you post will help you or hinder you in framing and creating your narrative.

Fun with Filters

Instagram provides some amazing filters to make your images really pop. You can take a color photo and make it look more dramatic with a black and white filter, or you can make it look older with a sepia filter. You can even soften the colors or brighten the image.

One thing to remember, however, is that random and mindless use of filters can look sloppy and unprofessional. By using only one or two filters consistently, you will help the viewer see your feed as a mosaic rather than individual shots.

Variety is the Spice of Instagram

If all you post are selfies or glamorous professional shots, your feed can feel stagnant and boring. Be sure to vary your posts to engage your followers in different ways. Selfies set one tone, while professional shots set another. Likewise, abstract and artsy images set one tone, while a wide angle shot sets yet another. Be sure to mix things up. Too many of any one kind of image can get boring to the viewer.

The Theory of Instagram Relativity

Take a moment to imagine a rose. See it clearly in your mind's eye. Now imagine that rose being held by a bride as she walks down the aisle. Notice the emotions that image evokes. Now imagine the same rose resting on a casket as it is being lowered into a grave. Again, notice the emotions that rose evokes.

The reason you can have very different emotional reaction to the same rose is because the human brain perceives things through the lens of relativity. In other words, you are not seeing a rose. You are seeing a rose relative to the things around it. The meaning of the rose is heavily influenced by the setting in which it is placed.

This same principle not only applies to the individual photographs and videos you post, but also to the photos posted before and after. Your Instagram feed, for better or worse, invites your followers to have their perception informed by all of the images in your feed—especially the ones just before and just after.

If you are mindful of this principle, you can use it to your advantage. If you forget this principle, you may well find that people are reacting to your posts in unintended ways that do not serve you as a teacher or healer.

Facebook Marketing and Instagram

Because Facebook purchased Instagram, the two platforms work very well together. The most obvious example of this is in Facebook pay-per-click marketing.

When you run an ad on Facebook, you can run the same ad on Instagram at the same time. This makes advertising a breeze, but a quick word of caution: the ads that work on Facebook may not lend themselves to Instagram. Be sure to monitor your analytics and modify ads for each platform accordingly.

Conclusion

A few short years ago, nobody really knew what social media was. But thanks to Twitter, Facebook, and a plethora of other social networks that have sprung up in recent years, the world has again become much smaller. We have the ability to reach out and network with people in a very targeted way. People who are likely to appreciate the work we do and benefit from the healing and teaching we offer can easily be discovered and, hopefully, become regular students and clients.

The best part about social media is it combines the things we do best with the things we need to do to succeed. As teachers and healers, what we do best is connect with those we serve. We provide an opportunity for healing and growth. We do this by forming relationships. Still, many of us resist social media. We see it as taking away from our healing and teaching work rather than extending it. I hope this book has shown you that this doesn't need to be the case. You can use social media as a natural part of the healing work you do. It just needs to be done in a mindful and intentional way.

Many of us work on a very limited marketing budget, so the money and time we do invest in our marketing efforts needs to be well considered. Here, again, social media provides us with an amazing opportunity to reach new students and clients at a fraction of the cost it once would have taken.

Better still, we can target the students who are most likely to appreciate our work. We can meet new people and network with other professionals, and we can excite people about the work we do long before they meet us in person. Our existing clients and students can stay motivated and maintain excitement about the benefits of the work we offer. All of this takes just a small amount of time each week. With the proper planning, the right strategy, and modern technology, we can engage with our social media platforms quickly and easily and reap amazing benefits.

Starting or growing a social media presence takes work, so give yourself a few months to really dive deep. Commit to two hours a week to implement a well-considered plan, use analytics to see what works and what doesn't, and notice if your efforts result in new and more energized clients. If you put forth the effort, you will see results far beyond what you may have imagined.

I hope you enjoyed this book and found it helpful. I know it didn't answer all of your questions about social media, but I do hope it offered some valuable tools, insights, and perspective.

I hope you will take a moment to review this book on Amazon and Audible and join our Facebook community, The Yogi Entrepreneur. While I can't answer every question promptly, I do respond frequently to questions posted in the Facebook group and to messages sent to me through my website, www.DarrenMain.com

I look forward to seeing you on social media and hearing about the great success you achieve!

Namaste,
Darren
www.darrenmain.com

Resources Mentioned
in This Book

Below are some of the resources mentioned in this book. The Yogi Entrepreneur Resource Guide, has additional resources and can be downloaded for free at www.darrenmain.com.

Some of the links listed below are to services with which I have an affiliate relationship. Whenever possible, I have negotiated a discount for readers of this book.

The Yogi Entrepreneur Facebook Group
www.facebook.com/groups/YogiEntrepreneur

Dashboards to Manage Your Social Media
Buffer- www.buffer.com
Hootsuite- www.hootsuite.com
Manage Filter- https://goo.gl/mtvauY
Social Oomph- https://goo.gl/SxaBKH

Curate Content
Feedly- www.feedly.com
Reddit- www.reddit.com
YouTube-www.YouTube.com

Other Resources
MailChimp- http://eepurl.com/cT4gNr

Udemy Online Learning-

Zoom Video Conferencing- http://bit.ly/2pJgKA6

Appointlet Scheduler- https://goo.gl/mw6sd5

Fiverr for Outsourcing -

https://www.fiverr.com/s2/f798777225

Acknowledgements

Special thanks to the family and friends who have supported me in my writing this book and to my son, Jaden Main, who is my greatest source of inspiration. A big thanks to Jesse Winter and Beth Foley for your sharp editor's eye.

Books by Darren Main

Yoga and the Path of the Urban Mystic
Amazon | Audible

The Yogi Entrepreneur: A Guide to Earning a Mindful Living Through Yoga
Amazon | Audible

Inner Tranquility: A Guide to Seated Meditation
Amazon | Audible

Spiritual Journeys along the Yellow Brick Road
Amazon | Audible

River of Wisdom: 108 Life-Changing Reflections
Amazon

Hearts & Minds: Talking to Christians about Homosexuality
Amazon | Audible

Made in the USA
Monee, IL
10 February 2021